JESUS FOR A SECULAR AGE?

Also by Leslie Scrase:

Days in the Sun (children's stories, with Jean Head)
In Travellings Often
Booklet on Anglican/Methodist Conversations
Some Sussex and Surrey Scrases
Diamond Parents
The Sunlight Glances Through (poetry)
Some Ancestors of Humanism
An Evacuee
Conversations (on Matthew's Gospel)
　　　　between an Atheist and a Christian
A Prized Pupil!
A Reluctant Seaman
The Game Goes On (poetry)
It's Another World
A Talented Bureaucrat
Town Mouse and Country Mouse (nature diary)
More from the Country Mouse (nature diary)
Kenneth and Bob (children's story)
Letting off Steam (short essays)
Scribblings of an old romantic (poems)
Happy Endings (short stories)
An Unbeliever's Guide to the Bible
The Four Gospels Through an Outside Window
　　　　　　– A Commentary
Autobiography of a Blockhead (poetry)
Postscript (poetry)
Belief, Unbelief, Ethics and Life
Driven Crazy – My Life with Cars & Other Vehicles
Infamous Last Words (poetry)
Footprints in the Sand (poetry)
A Late Harvest (poetry)
Coping With Death (4th Edition)
An Unknown Poet Sings

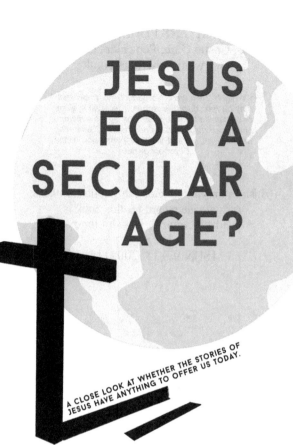

JESUS FOR A SECULAR AGE?

A CLOSE LOOK AT WHETHER THE STORIES OF JESUS HAVE ANYTHING TO OFFER US TODAY.

Leslie Scrase

UNITED WRITERS
Cornwall

UNITED WRITERS PUBLICATIONS LTD
Ailsa, Castle Gate, Penzance, Cornwall.
www.unitedwriters.co.uk

British Library Cataloguing in Publication Data:
A catalogue record for this book is
available from the British Library.

ISBN 9781852002114

Printed and bound in Great Britain by
United Writers Publications Ltd.,
Cornwall.

To Helen and Alison
for their encouragement
and to Nelly Moïa.

Acknowledgements

Once again I want to express my gratitude to Malcolm Sheppard of United Writers Publications. Everyone who knows me knows that my typing is awful. That is now compounded by a very sick typewriter which lacks punctuation and the odd letter. Out of such chaos Malcolm produces perfect copy. I'm very thankful.

Contents

(Most Biblical quotations are from the New English Bible.)

Chapter 1

Where Ignorance is Bliss

One of my brothers taught Latin at a fee-paying Grammar school.

One Friday afternoon his last two lessons were a double Latin for the lower sixth form. He presented the students with a story in Latin and told them to translate it into English.

'When you have finished, hand in your books and you can go home. But if you recognise the story, simply write its title across the page, show me, and you can go home early.'

Time passed. The best and fastest Latin students completed their work and went home. Others toiled away, handed in their work and went home, until at last they had all completed their work.

None of them recognised the story. It was new to them all. Yet all of their parents were reasonably well-heeled and most of them would probably have called themselves 'Christian'. And the boys and girls themselves had endured a whole school life-time of compulsory religious education. Yet none of them recognised the parable of the Good Samaritan, one of the most famous of all the stories told by Jesus.

Does it matter?

My own education was quite specifically Christian. I grew up knowing nothing of the teachings of Hinduism, the Buddha, or Confucius, the ancient Greek philosophers or Muhammad. Why would I when it was a Christian who closed down Plato's famous Academy in Athens after centuries of academic service.

Did it matter?

Do any or all of these teachers really have anything to say so many centuries later? And in particular, do religious thinkers and teachers have anything to say to people in a secular age, people who are living perfectly happily without religion of any kind?

If they do, I think it will be in the fields of ethics and morality. Good and evil do not change. They are the same in every age and for every generation. Ancient teachers, whether religious or not, were all concerned with the way we should live our lives. That is what makes them relevant today.

Insofar as Jesus was concerned with that question he may still have valuable lessons to teach us. But to arrive at the useful things he had to say we have to strip off a great deal of myth, a great deal that is now meaningless.

Chapter 2

The Churches

We owe our knowledge of the life and teachings of Jesus to the existence of the Christian churches. They, in their turn, owe their existence primarily to two people and to two nations.

The two people are Jesus himself and the other dominant figure of the New Testament, the apostle Paul. It was Paul who was the first to recognise that the message of Jesus was of universal value. It was not just a message to Jews. It belonged to non-Jews as well. But for that recognition, Jesus would probably have been lost in the mists of a fairly insignificant history. For Jesus and his religion have never made much headway amongst the Jews.

In point of fact, wherever in the world there was a well developed religion or philosophy or ethical system, Christianity has never made much headway. India and China are two obvious examples.

But the religions of Europe were not very satisfying. Once the God of the Jews was separated from the nation of the Jews, he began to widen his appeal. (Forgive me for using the masculine form throughout this book. I do know that God, if God exists, is neither he nor she but Spirit –

unless, of course, Jesus is God, in which case – oh dear – now we really are in trouble!)

Before we leave the Jews we must notice two ways in which the infant church played piggy-back. First of all it took the holy books of the Jews for its own Bible – the Word of God. During the first centuries of its life it added twenty-seven books of its own, including the four gospels on which we depend for our knowledge of Jesus.

Secondly, it learned how to organise itself by learning from the Jews of the Dispersion. Long before the coming of Jesus, the Jews had been conquered by the Assyrians and the Babylonians. Each time, their leading people were carried off into exile. Many of these exiles never returned, but they didn't just merge with their captors and lose their identity.

Aided by their superior religion, they stuck to one another, built synagogues and began a system of weekly worship, bringing them all together and cementing the bonds between them within one religion and one national family. They set a pattern which Jews far from Israel have never lost.

When Paul and others began to try to spread the new Christian message, they began in the synagogues. Unwelcome and unsuccessful there, they used the Jewish genius for organisation themselves. They established their own places – churches – as places for weekly worship and as places for binding one another together into one family. Soon there was a loosely linked confederation of groups of people connected solely by their attachment to their missionary teacher and the teachings of Jesus, with their headquarters in Jerusalem.

Thus far then, the existence of Christianity has been down to two people (there were rather more than just these two) and one nation: Jesus, Paul and the Jews. Now it was the turn of the Romans to play a major part in the future development of Christianity and the churches. This began with the destruction of Jerusalem and its temple. This ended the Jewish role in the development of Christianity and led, in time, to the pre-eminence of Rome.

But it was the conversion of a Roman Emperor – Constantine – which was to transform the fortunes of the Christians. Supported by the largest empire in the western world, Christianity became the official religion of the empire and developed the incredible panoply of pomp and style – not to say wealth – that has marked parts of the church ever since.

The conversion of Constantine and the transformation of the life of the church, led to a new strategy. Not only did the church learn to play piggy-back on imperial spread and growth (something it was to do with later empires), but it also learned to target the top people.

Convert the top people, win an alliance with a head of state or of a tribe, and the whole nation or tribe was yours. It was this strategy which led to the spread of Christianity throughout Europe. And later, as European empires spread throughout the world, Christianity played the same game in the Americas, in Africa, Australia and New Zealand or simply used military force to make its way.

Of course, a converted head of state may not have had any real understanding of the new religion, and his or her people may have been almost completely ignorant of its teaching, but given time and the backing of the powerful, the church could make its way.

And yet another strategy helped. The church learned to take on board as many of those beliefs already held in the area as they could. Festivals were Christianised. Special days were turned into saint's days. And the widespread belief in sacrifice was purified and ennobled by concentration on Jesus as the one, pure and perfect sacrifice for the sins of the world.

Tragically, the newfound power and authority of the church led it astray. It began to use the weapons of power. Not all Christians had quite the same beliefs about Jesus. That part of the church which had its headquarters in Rome began to try to call the tune for all other Christians. It began to persecute Christians with different ideas of the meaning of their religion. Dissidents were suppressed with great cruelty and ferocity. But the Roman church overplayed its hand and the church as a whole began to splinter into a host of different churches, beginning with the major split between west and east: the Roman and Orthodox churches. Here in England and in West Europe, we are more familiar with the Protestant reformation which began with Martin Luther and is now represented by a host of splinter groups – a few of them very large splinters. Some of these have also used persecution, torture, and murder (burning at the stake) to enhance their authority.

I wonder what Jesus would make of the churches he has spawned. John's Gospel has his prayer that his followers 'may be one, even as I and the Father are one.'

There are magnificent buildings putting the old Jewish Temple in the shade. Built to impress and dominate, many of them are just tourist attractions and white elephants now. Those who built them lived in homes little better than hovels, and didn't live long. There also plenty of 'Pharisees and Sadducees' about too but I must not be too over-critical. Churches large and small are also home to a host of thoroughly decent people and devoted clergy. There is some fine teaching too, although it still sits alongside the most incredible and pathetic kinds of superstition. Think, for example, of weeping statues and of the so-called 'holy oil' used at the recent coronation.

In my lifetime, the churches have been steadily losing their grip on society. Although countries like England still have a facade of religion for state occasions, that has much more to do with people's love of spectacle than of any real belief in any of the churches' teachings. On the whole the church has become irrelevant. It certainly no longer has the power to frighten people into its fold, and only rarely to win strangers to its teaching. This is obvious when you look at all the closed churches and chapels and see the reduction in services at the places that remain.

But, in spite of everything, the churches are still the heirs of the teaching of Jesus. Our understanding of that teaching still comes from the churches and from the four gospels in which it is enshrined.

Chapter 3

The Birth of Jesus

In Shakespeare's 'Henry IV' Glendower boasts of all the amazing things that happened when he was born:

'The front of heaven was full of fiery shapes, of burning comets, and at my birth the frame and huge foundation of the earth shak'd like a coward. . .' and so on.

Hotspur mocks him: 'Why, so it would have done at the same season, if your mother's cat had but kitten'd. . .'

People used to like to associate cosmic happenings with the birth of the great men of the world. The birth of Jesus was no exception. But we actually know very little about it that is factual.

Nobody knows when Jesus was born, in spite of Luke's Gospel trying to date it fairly precisely. Christian scholars now reckon that Jesus was born somewhere between 6 and 4 BCE.

We can take it as almost certain that Jesus was not born on Christmas Day. The Christmas festival is simply another example of the Church taking over the festivals of other religions and turning them to their own advantage.

If we know anything about the birth of Jesus, we shall find the information in the four gospels. The first of them was written between sixty and seventy years after Jesus was born. That was Mark's Gospel. Mark doesn't mention the birth of Jesus at all. He begins his story with Jesus as an adult seeking baptism by John the Baptist.

Matthew and Luke's Gospels came next. If we begin with Luke we shall find him beginning with the birth of John the Baptist and the conception of Jesus by an unmarried young woman called Mary. There is a family relationship between the two mothers to be and Mary visits and stays with Elizabeth. A story full of angels, it is beautifully and simply told, and both Mary and John's father Zechariah burst into poetry.

It is clear that both children are destined to be important.

Luke tried to pin down the date of Jesus' birth to the date of 'the first registration. . . when Quirinius was governor of Syria'. This is also used to explain why people from Nazareth should be in Bethlehem at the time of the birth. What follows is significant in a number of ways:

'Mary was betrothed to Joseph.' Betrothed or married? They did marry but they were not married when Jesus was conceived. The claim was made that Mary conceived by the Holy Spirit (the third person of the Christian Trinity). But setting that on one side, I can't help wondering why it is that the church has always been so hard on unmarried mothers – only the mothers, not the fathers. This callous cruelty continued into my adult life. Only my grandchildren's generation put an end to the cruelties and stigma of the past.

The second thing to notice is that Luke called Jesus Mary's *first-born* son. Throughout the gospels there are references to the four brothers and to 'all' the sisters of Jesus. What then are we to make of the ridiculous claims of some of the churches that Mary remained a virgin for the rest of her life? That is the only real 'Blessed Assumption' that is made about Mary.

Thus far we have the birth of Jesus to Mary (and Joseph) in Bethlehem somewhere between 6 and 4 BCE.

In Luke's Gospel the birth is followed by the story of angels visiting shepherds and of the shepherds visiting the baby.

It is one of the familiar, lovely Christmas stories and it is told as if it actually happened. For those of us who do not believe either in God or in angels, it is simply a lovely story. If we turn back to Matthew's Gospel we shall find another story, but this one has a terrible ending.

Matthew traced the ancestry of Jesus through Joseph to King David, which is meaningless if Joseph was not the boy's father. Luke traced Jesus' ancestry back to Adam, who, of course, never lived!

Having told us that Jesus was born during the reign of Herod the king, Matthew goes on to tell the famous story of the visit of the Magi – astrologers. Again it is told as if it were factual but it is as fanciful as most astrology and it leads to horror.

The association of the Magi with Herod led to 'the massacre of all children in Bethlehem and its neighbourhood, of the age of two or less.' Fortunately for Jesus, Joseph had been forewarned by an angel and gone to Egypt and safety. So God was quite happy to intervene on behalf of Jesus and to let the other children die. What sort of a God is this?

Although Herod was quite capable of instituting a massacre, and although Jesus has been associated with so much unnecessary death down through the centuries, my own take on this is that once more we have a story aimed at pointing the significance of the birth of Jesus – a story: Only a story.

When we come to the end of the life of Jesus it will be important to remember these stories – stories told as if they were factual, but simply stories, not more.

In Luke there is another story and this one will certainly be based on fact. Luke told the story of the circumcision of Jesus in Jerusalem, and of two fine people making a great deal of fuss of this special child. People do like to make a fuss of babies and Jesus will certainly have been circumcised.

Before we leave the birth of Jesus it is important that we turn to John's Gospel, the last of the four to be written and quite different in its approach. John gives us none of the facts or stories we have had in Matthew and Luke. Instead, in a beautifully written and carefully thought out chapter, John gives us a picture of Jesus as 'the Word of God.'

Here, spelt out, is the claim that Jesus is more than just a very special man. Put at its simplest, this chapter claims that Jesus is God – later to be defined as the second person in the Christian Trinity. Paul's letter to the Colossians makes the same claim in a different way.

If Jesus is God, it follows that he must be absolutely perfect – perfect God and perfect man. But the gospels show very clearly that, whatever qualities Jesus had as a man, he was not perfect. It follows that he is not God either.

In point of fact a man cannot be God. God cannot be reduced to sperm fertilising a woman's egg; God cannot grow tired, let alone irritable (no not even with me as I write these things). God does not curse fruit trees. God cannot die. Nor can he take my place as a sacrifice to himself.

My own view is that John has been looking at the Greek

and Roman gods, gods who behave very much as humans do only more so. John has attempted to portray the divine/human interaction in a much more sophisticated way – a very beautiful way for those who can believe it. And having claimed that Jesus is God the Word, he will go on to report that Jesus made a series of immense claims for himself leading finally to the claim 'I am the resurrection and the life.'

The claim that Jesus is the second person of the Trinity means everything to many thinking Christians and it has led to some magnificent poetry and music. But the complexities of the theology which arises from this concept are far too much for most of us. And in the end, we have to ask, if religious teaching cannot be understood, what is its value?

Those of us who do not believe in God have no problem at all. If there is no God, Jesus is not God. And since there is no such thing as a perfect man, he was not a perfect man either. It really is as simple as that.

So what do we know of the birth of this man?

Very little.

He was probably born between 6 and 4 BCE. At his conception, his mother was not married but it looks as though she married the man who was the actual father. If not born in Bethlehem, he would have been born in the family home town of Nazareth and he was circumcised according to Jewish law and custom. More than that we cannot say.

If Jesus is to have any significance for a secular age, it will be found in his life and teachings.

Chapter 4

The Spark that Lit the Flame

Almost nothing is known of the childhood and youth of Jesus, except that he was the eldest member of a pretty large family. There is one story in Luke's Gospel about him as a twelve year old. His parents had taken him to Jerusalem for the Passover festival. It is clear that a lot of people went every year – friends and relations.

On this occasion, when the festival was over and they all set off for home, Jesus remained behind. Clearly a precocious boy, and very much a typical twelve year old wrapped up in his own thoughts, he stayed in the Temple asking questions of the rabbis there. He impressed them with his seriousness and thoughtfulness. His questions were real and they enjoyed trying to help his thinking forward. He never gave a thought to his parents.

Meanwhile, when they finally realised that he wasn't among the boys of his age, that in fact he was missing, they went back to Jerusalem to search for him. Where on earth would a twelve year old boy be?

The story claims that it took them three days to find him. Perhaps that's a bit of an exaggeration, but at last they found him in the Temple. With the typical self-centred blindness of a boy, he says: 'What made you search? Did you not know that I was bound to be in (the Temple) my Father's house?'

I remember a clergyman's wife commenting, 'If he had been my son I'd have beaten him.'

His parents didn't beat him but he did go back with them to Nazareth where 'he advanced in wisdom and in favour with God and men.'

And nothing more is known of him until he was about thirty years old.

It was then that his cousin John, who became known as John the Baptist, began his prophetic ministry. John was an austere figure with the kind of hell-fire message that was still fairly common when I was growing up. Perhaps the best-known preacher of that ilk in my lifetime was Ian Paisley in Northern Ireland, but there were plenty of priests and nuns on the other side of the Christian divide whose message was just as grim, full of the fires of hell.

But John's message was also a call to lives of high ethical value.

John spoke bluntly both to his fellow Jews and also to the soldiers of the occupying Roman army. 'No bullying; no blackmail,' and to everyone live generously: share what you have.

John's ministry seems to have been the spark that ignited Jesus. Perhaps he felt that his family didn't need him any more. If John could become a prophet was he also being called to some sort of special ministry?

He went to see John and was baptised by him. It is clear that he was a man of some quality. John respected him – even felt that he was the better man of the two. No doubt they held some pretty long intense conversations with one another.

And then Jesus went off 'into the wilderness' to be on his own and to think about the kind of ministry he felt he ought to follow.

Should he be a kind of social worker trying to help people escape from poverty? No. There is more to life than the struggle with poverty (tell that to those who are actually in poverty): 'Man cannot live on bread alone, he lives on every word that God utters.'

So should he try to impress people with a host of signs and wonders – miracles. Certainly not. The Word of God is far more important than the magic feats of passing entertainers.

Given all the stories of Jesus – a very compassionate Jesus – working miracles and feeding crowds, these decisions of his seem to have been decisions that could be over-ridden.

Finally he wrestled with these questions of status. Should he seek a revolutionary kind of ministry which would give him power and authority. He rejected that too – which makes his final challenge to the Jerusalem authorities all the more odd, tragic and pointless.

But his final decision about himself and his ministry lies in the words, 'You shall do homage to the Lord your God and worship him alone.'

He would spend his life seeking to know the will of God and to perform it.

Even an atheist like me can respect that. After all, we should all of us be trying to discover the best ways in which to live our lives, and we should spend all our energies in living as well as we possibly can.

The question is whether Jesus came up with anything helpful as we seek to fulfil that quest. It is high time that we looked at his actual ministry to see whether it has anything of value for a secular age.

Chapter 5

The Beginnings of the
Ministry of Jesus

We have seen that Jesus felt inspired by John the Baptist to begin special work of his own. We have also seen him going away to be on his own to work out what it was that he had to do.

Over the next two or three years he became (according to the gospels) a wandering teacher, healer and miracle worker.

I don't propose to look at the miracles at all although I won't guarantee that there will be no exceptions. My own view is that miracles don't happen. And even many Christians explain away some of the 'miracles' he did because they are uncomfortable with them.

Nor do I intend to spend time over the healings of Jesus. I am prepared to admit that Jesus may well have had some gifts in that direction, but even if all of the stories are absolutely true they have little to say to us today.

The churches have a very divided record when it comes to following his healing ministry. On the one hand, they often made a good deal of provision for people who were ill and gave them a good deal of care. But on the other hand, they resisted all attempts at studying illness in scientific

b

ways and often got in the way of advance.

But Jesus as a healer has no significance for a secular age, so we can leave the subject alone – with perhaps one parting shot. Whatever the truth behind his healings = there can be no doubt that there was a great deal of exaggeration. That becomes vividly clear when we look at the stories of Jesus raising people from death to life. Jesus himself is the one who provides disclaimers. Of Jairus' daughter Jesus said, 'she is not dead. She is asleep.' But after he roused her, people still claimed that he had raised her from the dead and they have been doing so ever since.

All of which brings us to Jesus the teacher.

All of the gospels paint a similar picture of the beginnings of the ministry of Jesus.

He gathers around him some of those who are to become his close companions and followers. And he goes home and preaches in the synagogue there.

At first people are delighted with him and proud of him. You can imagine a sort of groundswell of, 'Hasn't Joseph's son done well. Who would have thought it?' and so on. He excited the same kind of admiration as the first village school-child to win a place at a university.

But as soon as Jesus begins to make plain that he has outgrown his childhood and has a strong, stern message of his own, a message which is not afraid to be critical of his roots, the people turn against him pretty ferociously.

He also stirs up hostility when he begins to mix with social outcasts. 'Many bad characters were seated with him.' One of the attractive features of Jesus is precisely the fact that he had no side – he treated people of all ranks in society, from the highest to the lowest, in precisely the same way, with the same respect. But this doesn't alter the fact that he recognised that some people needed him more than others: 'It is not the healthy that need a doctor but the sick, I did not come to invite virtuous people, but sinners.'

I think that we should take careful note of this. Perhaps this whole book is completely irrelevant for most people. They don't need teachers to show them how to live. After all, most people are pretty decent, kind, and yes, virtuous. They don't need anyone to show them how to live or to make a fuss about the difference between right and wrong, good and bad. They already know. They learned from their parents who learned from their parents and so on and on and on through the generations.

According to the first three gospels (which are also the three earliest gospels) Jesus simply chose to wander around the towns and villages of northern Palestine with occasional excursions into neighbouring Samaria. Just how often he visited Jerusalem is open to discussion. John's Gospel has him visiting quite often and making his mark on his very first visit. The earlier gospels seemed to suggest that his only memorable visit to Jerusalem was right at the end of his travels.

It is interesting to look at that difference between them. If the first three gospels are correct, he simply wandered from town to town in Galilee and Samaria. Jerusalem hardly featured in his travels at all. But that picture troubled the author of John's Gospel. Such a wandering teacher would hardly have caused a ripple in the consciousness of the authorities. Imagine a wandering preacher in Wiltshire and Hampshire. He might feature occasionally on local radio or even TV but London would never get to hear of him. But John paints a picture of Jesus causing ructions in Jerusalem from the beginning – encouraged by his brothers. They had pointed out to him that if he wanted to make a name for himself, he needed to spend time in Jerusalem.

John also mentions that the brothers did not believe in him. What about 'All' his sisters? We know that the whole family was troubled about him early in his ministry. Why would his siblings believe in him? They knew him too well to believe the claims he began to make for himself. Joseph is never mentioned. Was he dead? And what of his mother? For her there could have been nothing but incomprehension and grief. Nor did Jesus behave very well towards them. When they came to see him with the hope that they might persuade him to go home, he completely ignored them – worse, he turned to the crowds all around him and told them you are my mother and father and family.

So much for his reminder that we should honour our parents.

But setting all of that on one side, what exactly was he trying to do? What was his plan? What were his aims? Did he have any or was he content in the early stages simply to be a wandering teacher? In the later stages we know that he developed different ideas, ideas involving himself as a sacrifice for the sins of men. But before all that, did he have any real sense of direction?

There is a brief paragraph where he speaks of the establishment of his church with Peter at its head (a Peter who was roundly condemned only a couple of minutes later). But what did he have in mind when he spoke of this church? Certainly it would have been nothing like the immense bureaucratic organisations that exist today, so far removed from him and his ministry and so often at variance with his teaching.

What was that teaching? Much of it is difficult to pin

down because it was given in response to questions or to the situations in which he found himself. It had no formal structure or plan. But in Matthew's Gospel it begins with the 'Sermon on the Mount' and the 'Beatitudes' so let us begin there.

Chapter 6

The Beatitudes

'The Sermon on the Mount' begins in Matthew chapter 5. It is not a real sermon. It is a collection of bits and pieces of the teaching of Jesus all thrown together from people's memories.

We should not underestimate those memories. They are much more developed in non-literate societies or recently literate, than in societies where reading has been common for a long time. I once gave a lecture to a class of young men in India and afterwards set them an essay on the general subject of my lecture. In essay after essay, back came my lecture. It looked vey much as though they had been cheating, copying the work of the cleverest of them. But they hadn't been cheating at all. They had been remembering what I had said and regurgitating it – sadly in an uncritical way, without thinking about it at all.

Both Matthew and Luke have a similar set of Beatitudes. Luke's is probably the more primitive. Matthew has turned his into a work of literature – one of the best loved pieces in the whole of the New Testament, loved and respected by no less a figure than Mahatma Gandhi. There is no doubt about its literary beauty, especially when you read it in the older translations of the gospels. But literary beauty and charm are not enough.

Lovely though the Beatitudes sound, most of them have nothing to say to us today. They offer nothing but what used to be called 'pie in the sky'. Those who are deprived or suffering in all sorts of different ways are told that they are 'blessed' because they will receive or enter the 'kingdom of heaven'.

If we look at the two which mean most to me, we shall begin to see just how inadequate or wrong they are:

'Blessed are those who mourn, for they shall be comforted.'

The statement is made but we are not told how they will be comforted or by whom. We simply have the bald statement, a statement that needs clarifying or justifying. On its own it is simply a meaningless promise. I can only add that, if readers are mourning as they read this, I hope that they will manage to find the comfort they need – from understanding family or friends, from the actual funeral, from helpful literature, and simply from their own inner resources.

The second Beatitude I want to look at reads, 'Blessed are the meek for they shall inherit the earth.' At the most basic level, that simply isn't true. It is the strong, the arrogant, the wealthy, who inherit the earth and fence it off and placard it with notices saying 'Trespassers will be prosecuted'. Sadly, so many of these people have little or no appreciation of all that they possess.

The only sense in which the meek really do inherit the earth is in their appreciation of all that is around them; their own little plot or the things they can see and experience when out for a stroll – often when looking over the fence of the arrogant and wealthy, looking at the view, or enjoying animals, birds and flowers – many of which live and grow just where they will, regardless of man's possessiveness. But Jesus does not offer these delights. Here he only offers the Kingdom of Heaven – a future and mythical bliss beyond the grave.

The rest of the Beatitudes follow much the same pattern. Jesus says that those who 'hunger and thirst' will see right prevail and will be satisfied. And he says that mercy will be shown to those who show mercy. Neither of these things is true. The hungry often go hungry to their graves. And where mercy should be shown, it is often lacking.

Jesus goes on to speak of 'those whose hearts are "pure" and of 'peacemakers'. Needless to say, we should be thankful for both groups of people, but Jesus goes on to speak of the rewards they will receive in heaven. In so doing he spoils everything. Quite apart from the meaningless nature of those rewards, virtue, decency and good work are all their own reward. It is not people who live their lives for the rewards they can earn who are virtuous and admirable, but those who live well because that is the right and proper way to live. These things *are* reward in themselves. Where we know that we have done something worthwhile, the joy and satisfaction that brings is more than sufficient.

Finally, I see no joy in suffering persecution even for the cause of right. If the cause really is right we shall feel justified even if we are persecuted for our opinions and for the stand we have made, but that will be the limit of our joy. 'Insults and persecution and every kind of calumny' are not going to be made any easier to bear by talking of a 'rich reward in heaven.'

Luke ended his list of Beatitudes with a list of woes against the rich, the well-fed and those who are happy. There seems to be no specific reason for these woes and no reason to take the slightest notice of them. If they were part of the teaching of Jesus then he ought to have been ashamed of himself. The woes have no necessary justification at all.

Chapter 7

The Law

Apart from the stories he told, some of which we'll look at later, it is difficult to paint a coherent picture of the teachings of Jesus. It is as if we had been given some of the pieces of a hundred or so jig-saw puzzles and been asked to make one or two complete puzzles from them.

It is easy to pick out one piece and to write a sermon about it, whether that is a ten minute sermon or one of those to which we were subjected when I was young, lasting almost an hour. But it seems nigh on impossible to fit them all together into anything like an ordered whole.

Many of them have to do with the Jewish law – divine law given by God to Moses and therefore permanent and unchanging. There is also some reference to Roman law. Oddly enough, there were times when Roman law was more important than divine law as we shall see when we come to the crucifixion.

The scribes and Pharisees were nit-pickers obsessed with keeping every detail of the law. Again and again they criticise Jesus and his followers for minor infringements – even sometimes for major infringements – of the law. Jesus responds in a number of different ways.

He claims that his teaching takes precedence over the law – that he is above the law. And in a way, he even makes the same claim for us. He claims that the law was made for man and not man for the law, which means that human need takes precedence over the law.

In spite of these things, most of the time he tells us that we should keep the law and even go beyond its demands. He tells us that we must get behind the actual laws and try to find the spirit in which they were given. Keeping the spirit of the law is more important than keeping the letter of the law.

I was once involved in an amusing episode which demonstrates that. As I was driving into the east of Woking I noticed a police car behind me, so I drove very carefully all the way through Woking – no mean distance – making quite sure that I never exceeded the thirty mile an hour speed limit. As we drove out of the town the police pulled me over. They were furious. Couldn't I see what a tail-back I had caused?

I certainly could. Traffic galore was whizzing past accelerating hard now that the limit was passed. For once I was quite calm as I faced the police.

'If I had broken the speed limit you would have pulled me over and booked me for speeding. Now you are condemning me for keeping the law.'

It would have meant nothing to them if I had travelled at 35 or 40 miles an hour and claimed that I was following the spirit of the law rather than its letter.

But what of Jesus' claim that the law was made for man and not man for the law? If you have read Victor Hugo's novel 'Les Miserables', or seen the musical, you will know that it all revolves around a man who has broken the law and stolen in order to feed his family. Our sympathies are all with him. The sympathies of Jesus would also have been with him.

Would his sympathies have also been with those who manipulate the benefits system in order to make life a little bit easier for their families? I find it curious that those who come down hardest on such people are those who are comparatively wealthy and think nothing of their own tax avoidance.

Perhaps we should get back to the attitude of Jesus to the law. He claimed to be above the law; he claimed that human need takes priority over the law. What else?

In most of his teaching he tells people to keep both Jewish divine law and Roman secular law. Asked on one occasion whether it was right to pay taxes to Rome he caught out the questioners who were trying to trap him. If he said that it was right he would be unpopular with his own people who resented the Romans. If he said that there was no need to pay Roman taxes he would be in trouble with the Roman authorities.

He took a coin and asked his questioners whose head was on the coin. 'Caesar's' was the answer. 'Then give to Caesar the things that are Caesar's and give to God the things that are God's.'

It struck me as I was thinking about this again, that I never begrudged paying my taxes when I had respect for those who rule over us. But when our politicians show themselves to be quite unfit to be in any place of authority over us, then I would happily withhold my taxes. At the local level taxes seem much more appropriate because we can see the services provided as a result of the taxes we pay.

But what about giving God the things that are God's? If

there is no God, then there is no need to support churches or an expensive clergy. Instead we might feel more able to provide help and support to those organisations and individuals really in need.

In point of fact, in my life-time that seems to be precisely what has been happening. Released from the bonds of religion, we are much more free to use our resources for the good of those we really care about.

Once again I have allowed myself to be side-tracked. Jesus claimed to be above the law. He claimed that human need took precedence over the law. But he also instructed people over and over again to keep the law. And then he went one step further. As we have seen, he told us that we should try to get behind the law to the spirit of the law. There are all sorts of examples.

He speaks of those we have wronged. We should recognise our own wrongdoing and try to be reconciled before our victim brings down the full weight of the law upon us and we end up in jail.

He tells us always to try to sort out disagreements with other people without going to law if we possibly can and he goes into great detail to offer ways in which we can do this. Even though these things seem to be ordinary common sense, there seem to be large numbers of people who need this kind of advice, especially in America and increasingly in our own country.

But when Jesus talks about the old laws 'an eye for an eye and a tooth for a tooth' he goes way beyond common sense. He tells us not to set ourselves against those who wrong us but to forgive them. In the Lord's Prayer there is the plea 'Forgive us our trespasses as we forgive those who trespass against us.'

And when Peter asked how often we should forgive – 'as often as seven times?' Jesus told him that we should be much more extravagant and forgive up to seventy-seven times!

It is in the same vein that he told us to 'turn the other cheek'. Did I hear of someone or read of someone who followed Jesus' teaching to the letter! When someone hit him, he turned the other cheek and then flattened his opponent? There are times when the advice to turn the other cheek is thoroughly bad. In situations of domestic violence, the mouse who simply takes whatever is thrown, whether it is verbal or physical abuse, will never escape.

But there are also occasions when it is the best possible way to defuse an explosive situation.

Jesus also told people to 'love your enemies. Do good to those who hate you.' It is often not possible to do good to those who hate us because they won't accept any kind of overture from us. And to ask us to 'love' our enemies probably goes beyond the realms of possibility too. But we can step back from expressing our dislike or even hatred and we can avoid anything which may bring hatred to other people. Perhaps Jesus was only exaggerating for effect. Yet surely it is right to go to the limits of what is possible to try to accommodate other people and to avoid conflict with them?

Not content with these demands, Jesus said, 'You must be all goodness.' 'You must be perfect.'

Even if we think we are – perhaps especially if we think we are – none of us is perfect. But that doesn't mean that we shouldn't aim high. Wasn't it Robert Browning who said that it was better to aim high and fail than to aim low and succeed? No high jumper will get very far without setting the bar high.

Unfortunately, focussing on goodness can create a ghastly problem. It can lead into the pitfalls of self-satisfaction and pride. Just as Dickens' character Uriah Heap became obnoxious as an expression of a man who is self-consciously humble; so there is no one so uncomfortable to be with as the person who is self-consciously 'good' or what is worse, self-consciously good *and* pious. It is no wonder that Jesus told people not to make a parade of their religion and not to be hypocrites.

But in point of fact, we do not become good by trying to any more than we become happy by trying to be happy.

Whatever our life situation, if we simply get on with it, making the most of our opportunities and putting up with its stumbling blocks and always doing the very best we can, not only or even chiefly for ourselves but for all those with whom we come in contact, we shall discover to our surprise that we are happy – really happy. And although we may never get to know it, other people will begin to think of us as 'good' – good, decent, reliable, helpful, honest and kind.

Jesus suggested that the secret of goodness lay in being like little children. If we think of ourselves as little children we shall retain a quality of humility. He used the image of children fairly often when he wanted to persuade us not to think too highly of ourselves. If we can avoid soppy sentimentalism, the image is a good one but children are not saints! The image can only be taken so far. Jesus told us to be 'all goodness. . . perfect' but was not blind to our imperfections. When he went on to tell us not to pass judgement on other people nor to be critical of them, he said that we should always remember our own imperfections. So we should treat others as we would like them to treat us.

Sadly he didn't always set us a very good example. He

was scathing in his judgements on Pharisees and Sadducees who, after all, were not so very different from today's clergy – a pretty decent bunch of people on the whole. But his advice was sound. He put it in a very pithy way when he warned us not to try to take a speck out of someone else's eye when we had a great plank of wood in our own.

Another piece of advice he gave had a very practical bearing which is lost on us today. He told people to 'go the extra mile.'

Roman soldiers had the right to call on the services of any civilian to carry their packs, but only for one mile. Jesus told people to do what they were required to do, and then to go beyond the real requirements of the law. In point of fact, that is basically his attitude to law generally.

Be law abiding but look beyond the law to the spirit of the law. Taking the spirit of the law, go beyond its requirements and be the best that you can be. It is in a similar vein that he compared us to good servants, always alert and ready and also completely trustworthy. He had a lot to say about masters and servants. Although there are still plenty of masters and servants about, it is not a relationship that many of us would approve nowadays. But in point of fact, however we like to describe ourselves, whatever our position in society, whatever our standing in society, it is right that we should be challenged to be alert and ready to fulfil our given or chosen role and to do so with complete trustworthiness. This is perhaps even more important for those at the top of the pile than it is for those at the bottom.

Chapter 8

Don't Worry
(Matthew 6, 25 – 34)

This is one of the favourite passages in the whole of the New Testament so I criticise it at my peril. And yet its popularity is very curious because it is so completely wrong in so many ways.

Perfect Jesus wrong?

I'm afraid so.

And yet, at first sight, he seems so right. 'Don't worry.' Surely that is excellent advice.

As it stands, no I don't think it is excellent advice. Worry is like the red light which is used to tell us that something is going wrong. It is a signal to us to stop what we are doing before we get into a mess.

What is excellent advice is the advice 'Don't *go on* worrying.'

Now that is excellent advice, but quite useless of course. Some people seem to be temperamentally unable to stop worrying. Others seem to be temperamentally unable to start! My father used to come home from work and pour out his troubles to my mother. Then he would go to bed and sleep like a log while she would lie awake half the night worrying about things she couldn't influence in any way – ending up giving herself ulcers.

It is not enough to tell worriers not to worry. They have to learn how to deal with their worries. When that red light worry flashes, we need to sit down quietly and analyse the causes of it. And then we need to work out ways in which to deal with what is wrong. Once we have done that and put the wrong things right, then we can stop worrying.

So we have to learn to welcome worry as a red warning light. But then, like a mechanic with a car, we discover what is going wrong and find ways to put things right.

Continuing to worry achieves nothing. Dealing with our worries gets rid of them.

Jesus realised that it wasn't enough just to say 'Don't worry.' His solution was to say that God provides everything we need. Now let us assume for a moment that there is a God. Even then, Jesus was only right at the most basic level. His God has provided a world with all the fossil fuels we need if we can find them – all the fossil fuels we need to destroy the world. And his God has provided all the food and drink we need as long as we don't go on reproducing and multiplying at such a rate. I'm a fine one to talk with four children and umpteen grandchildren.

'Don't worry,' did he say?

Of course we should worry about climate change, but only in the sense that we should recognise it and sit down quietly and find the ways to deal with it and then actually do what is necessary. And that is precisely what we have done up to the point where we have found what we need to do. Actually doing what is necessary is a different matter because it leads along so many paths that don't win votes at elections.

It is up to us. We can either set out to save the world or we can destroy it. In the end it is as simple as that.

But what is the use saving it if we are going to allow the population to grow to such an extent that we can't feed it? Because the simple and blunt truth is that the God of Jesus hasn't provided enough for all the millions of us there are.

Always there is famine somewhere – usually in Africa. There are just too many humans in spite of our readiness to kill one another and to destroy other species and the world they depend on.

There are United Nations figures which seem to suggest that we are beginning to learn the population message. Has human population peaked already or is that soon to take place – with all the attendant problems of an ageing population?

How curious it is that those parts of the world where we are learning to limit our population now need immigrants from those parts of the world that still haven't learned – immigrants we are still trying to turn away from our shores! It is all so complicated and confusing. Aged nearly 92 as I write 'I'm all right, Jack', but who is going to pay my grandchildren's pension without immigration – always assuming that they have a world to live in.

Don't worry? Of course we should worry with all those red lights shining. But we should only worry enough to find solutions and to work to put those solutions in place.

Work?

No, said Jesus. You don't have to work. 'Look at the birds of the air; they do not sow and reap. . . Consider how the lilies grow in the fields – they do not work, they do not spin. . .'

How incredibly wrong Jesus was.

I'm sorry, but that is the simple truth. Just walk around your garden. Try growing a few flowers or some vegetables. Your plants won't grow unless they put out roots and seek the nutrients and the rainwater in the soil – and sometimes you will have to provide extra nutrients or extra water because your God has not provided enough or he has not provided it at the right times.

And what of the birds of the air? It is true that they do not sow or reap but by golly they don't half have to work hard to feed their chicks. Find someone who knows about birds. Sit down with that somebody for an hour or two near to a blue-tit's nest and watch the comings and goings of the parents as they try desperately to feed their growing family. No humans ever work so hard – ever could work so hard.

This beautiful and moving passage of scripture is so completely up the creek – but at least it has suggested to me the need to write this chapter and to try to find the right message for our own secular age.

When the red light of worry goes on – Stop. Sit down quietly on your own or with other worried people. Work out what is wrong and what needs to be done to put things right. And last of all, and most important of all, do the things that are necessary to put right what is wrong.

After all that, I think I'll take my electric car in for servicing.

Chapter 9

Swearing

As a child at home, the strongest cuss word I ever heard came from my mother: 'Oh bother!' It wasn't until I went to school and began to get an education that I learned other words beginning with 'b' – one of them being so wonderfully expressive but with a completely unmentionable meaning. These were words never to be used. One of my brothers taught us to say 'oh sugar' instead.

And finally I went to a Christian boarding school where the English master taught us that the use of swear words demonstrated a deficiency in our knowledge and ability in the English language. When we became prefects, expected to set a good example, we had a 'swear box' in the prefects' room. If we swore, we were expected to put a penny in the box. I don't think I ever had to contribute.

And then, called up to do National Service in the Navy, suddenly I was in a different world. Two of us once timed a normal conversation between two other fellow recruits. In the space of one minute, the 'f' word was used ninety times. Clearly this was not really swearing. This was just normal English usage for a section of the population we had never met before.

Jesus said, 'You are not to swear at all.' Is this then what the significance of Jesus is reduced to?

Far from it. In the same part of Matthew's Gospel he spoke of the law, personal relationships, adultery, murder. And when he told us not to swear, he was not talking about our use of language or of cussing and swearing. He was talking about the use of oaths to try to convince people of our seriousness and integrity.

'You are not to swear at all – not by heaven, nor by. . .' 'Plain "Yes" or "No" is all you need to say.' In other words, a man of integrity has no need to back up his statements by swearing oaths. His 'word is his bond'.

It was the Quakers who picked up on this and who won for all of us the right to refuse to swear on the Bible in court – something for which many of us are grateful. What is the point of swearing on the Bible. The honest man will speak the truth without needing to swear an oath. The dishonest man (unless he is deeply superstitious) will lie no matter how many oaths he has sworn.

So what Jesus was really concerned with was our integrity. And that is something which matters in every age. If we are men and women of integrity we can be trusted and it will be a pleasure to do business with us.

But if we cannot be trusted, then we are worthless whether as business associates, friends or companions. Integrity is a vital ingredient| of human life. Without it, normal decent human life is impossible. Jesus was right and so were the early Quakers.

Chapter 10

Sex and Marriage

Jesus, his apostle Paul, and the Christian Church have all joined together to turn our sexual feelings from something that can be very beautiful and wonderful into something nasty, dirty, unspeakable and vile. And in the hands of many within the church it has become precisely those things. Where it all began I'm not sure. Certainly Paul was one of those responsible. He taught that sex was only for those who lacked the strength of will to stay celibate.

Was that the beginning or was it all the rubbish about Mary being a virgin. The gospels themselves tell us that Mary had a minimum of seven children: Jesus, four named brothers, and an unspecified number of sisters. Yet, instead of making Mary the heroine of all unmarried mothers, the church turned her into a virgin and demonised all who, like her, conceived children out of wedlock. Worse. In my lifetime the church did all it could to persuade mothers to part with their babies.

So, the Christian ideal was virginity for women and celibacy for men. Marriage was always only a second best. As a result celibacy was required of the clergy. From popes downwards that has always resulted in a large number of illegitimate babies being born. So why on earth did the church always demonise 'bastards' and penalise them for the 'sins' of their parents? In some centuries wandering friars became notorious as a danger to married women. And in our own time the evils perpetrated in church schools and other church institutions have become notorious, with the church trying very hard to cover up the harm they have done and to protect their own.

It is a sad, sick story. And when we turn from sex to marriage things are only marginally better. So let us begin with the best.

The Christian ideal marriage is of one man and one woman together for life. As far as it goes that is a fine ideal. But like so many of our ideals, it is something many of us fail to achieve. As I write I am over forty years into my second marriage so I'm a failure.

When you read about the antics of many Greeks and Romans in ancient times, you can well understand why Christians developed the ideal they still uphold. I prefer it to either the Islamic or the Mormon approach but, of course, the LBG community will not be happy with it. It is good that in so many areas they have managed to get rid of old laws, old cruelties, and have won for themselves so many 'rights' that they should never have had to fight for in the first place. They have had a long, hard battle and their main opponent has always been the Christian church. And even now, it is the Christian church which stands in the way of their proper, simple acceptance within society.

But let us return to the subject of marriage between a man and a woman. The Christian ideal is that the union is lifelong. Where that ideal is achieved it is both lovely and laudable. We honour those who achieve a genuinely happy relationship that lasts. But the Christian church has always made it difficult for those who do not achieve that ideal. And for that, Jesus is partly responsible.

Somebody once asked him, 'Is it lawful for a man to divorce his wife?' He said to them, 'Whoever divorces his wife and marries another commits adultery against her; so too, if she divorces her husband and marries another, she commits adultery.'

You couldn't have anything more straightforward than that, and the Roman Catholic church still operates on that basis. It doesn't recognise divorce and it will not remarry divorced people. Although even the Catholic church can sometimes find ways around what seems to be a simple set of rules, as Henry VIII well knew.

Many years ago a lady came to see me with her 'intended'. She was a Roman Catholic from birth. Her first marriage had given her four children but she was now divorced. She had been to see her priest to ask him to re-marry her.

He was a man who knew and respected her. He wanted to marry her to her new man and to keep her within his flock, but rules are rules, and these were pretty strict. However, there was a way out:

'If you tell me that your first marriage was never consummated then I can marry you.'

She was horrified. 'But you know my children. How could I possibly say such a thing when we both know that it isn't true?'

'If you tell me that your first marriage was never consummated, then I can marry you.'

She left him and in due course she came to see me. She and her new man were a fine couple, thoroughly decent people, and I was glad to be able to marry them.

c

These words of Jesus give all the churches problems. Mosaic law was supposed to be divine law and therefore binding for all time. Jesus was also supposed to be God. Therefore, if he gave his approval to the old Mosaic law, it had divine approval and was binding for all time.

But perhaps Mark has misquoted him? Or perhaps we should take into account the way in which Jesus behaved towards 'sinful' women. The churches wrestle with his bluntness in this passage and claim a little wriggle room. Some accept divorce and remarry under their own set of rules. The Church of England has chosen a pathway of sheer farce exemplified in the marriage of King Charles and Queen Camilla.

They were two divorcees so the church would not, could not, marry them. So they were married by the state. But what is a state marriage? Not a Christian marriage, that's for sure – not marriage in the sight of God, except that, of course, he sees everything! So then the Church blesses this non-Christian marriage in the name of God. If it weren't so sad, it would be laughable.

Meanwhile most of the rest of us are voting with our feet. Most of us, if we marry at all, do not go to churches to be married but find our own legal alternative.

Where sex and marriage are concerned, the church is completely out of touch. It has been responsible for a great deal that is evil and for a great deal of unnecessary pain and suffering. At best it is an ass. And all of that has its beginnings in Jesus.

Now that Charles and Camilla have become King Charles III and Queen Camilla, Charles is head of the church that refused to marry them! Not that that will change anything. He is a king without power. If ever we get rid of the monarchy I do so hope that we shall have the sense to have a President without power. Otherwise we might get landed with a Trump.

Chapter 11

Stories: Parables

Everybody loves a good story.

And Jesus has always been renowned for his stories. They were stories with a moral, of course. But he didn't point the moral as the Victorians did with a final sentence spoiling everything that had gone before. No, with his stories it was left to the listener to work out the moral. That would have been fine, except that his own disciples were so thick that they couldn't. They had to ask him to explain. 'What on earth was all that about?'

Of course, if you tell a story and leave it to your listeners to come up with a moral, they will not all come up with the same moral. And that is precisely the value of these stories for a secular age – apart from their simple value as stories. We do not have to come up with the same moral as Jesus did. Many, many years ago I took one of the stories of Jesus where he spoke of leaving the weeds in a field of wheat until harvest time and only separating the two then. There is a conventional interpretation but I chose to suggest a rather different one. I soon felt that my congregation was unhappy with my decision to move away from the old familiar interpretation.

It wasn't fair to take them out of the conventional rut and ask them to consider something new.

But for secular people, if the stories of Jesus are to have any value at all, it will be because they put their own interpretation on them, a this-worldly interpretation which has nothing to do with a kingdom of God or of heaven. And let's face it, many of the stories lend themselves to precisely this kind of explanation.

Take the first of them, the sower sowing his seed by hand. Farmers now sow their seed with machines carefully targeted and rationed so that there is no waste. But the gardener still sows by hand. He knows full well that if he is sparing, the seeds will get their own back by not coming up at all. And if he is generous, he will get so many plants that he won't know what to do with them. And yes, some will fall on the path, and some under the hedge and some where there are other plants and only a few in good open soil where they will enjoy the sun and the rain and flourish.

So as the gardener listens to the old story he will think of his own experience in the garden. Meanwhile the careful schoolteacher will think of all the preparation he has done for his class of stroppy fourteen or fifteen year old children. What a complete waste of time. Talk about waste ground – although you never know: Margaret and Wendy in row two, and Ted and Gordon a little further back, may be paying more attention than he realises. Yes, all that hard work may be worthwhile just for them.

Jesus told quite a lot of stories. Luke chapter fifteen has three of them, about loss and recovery. The first has a shepherd who has a hundred sheep and loses one of them. 'Does he not leave the ninety-nine in the open pasture and go after the missing one until he has found it?'

The second story is about a very special piece of silver lost from a bride's – how to describe it? – tiara would do. In India it would be from a bride's necklace. In England it would be her wedding ring. In other words what has been lost has a value far greater than its monetary worth. Does the bride not 'light the lamp, sweep out the house and look in every corner until she has found it?'

In both stories there is great focus on the joy of finding what was lost. Of course, for religious people these stories are all about sinners who are lost and the odd one here or there who is found.

But we don't need a promise of heaven to rejoice over the reformation of a really bad character or of a lost addict.

The third story is about a lost human, but oddly enough there is no evidence of reformation in this story. The story of 'the Prodigal Son' shows a younger son squandering his share of his father's wealth and ending up friendless and penniless. It dawns on him that he would be better off working at home as one of his father's servants. He can't expect that he will be welcomed home with much enthusiasm. In particular he knows that his steady, sensible, hard-working elder brother will not be pleased to see him. But he is pretty sure that his father will never turn him away, no matter how disappointed he is in him.

There is no evidence that he has any shame or remorse, any self-criticism. He simply knows what is good for him. And so he goes home and is welcomed with great joy by his father who welcomes his return home with an extravagant party. As he expected, his elder brother is both furious and very jealous.

The father points out that the younger son has had and squandered his inheritance. There is no going back on that.

Everything else will belong to the elder brother. But that doesn't alter the fact that the younger brother is home and his father is overjoyed to see him and to have him home again.

It is a lovely story and a pretty accurate portrayal of human beings as they are.

One of my own personal favourite stories is in Matthew's Gospel, chapter twenty. It is about a landowner hiring day labourers to work in his vineyard. It always makes me think of dockers a century or more ago. In the morning they would be at the dockyard gates hoping for work. The foreman would come out, having checked just how many workers he needed. His own family – perhaps a couple of sons or sons in law – would be the first to get jobs and then he would have his mates from the pub. And then he would look for the young and strong from among the rest until he had all the workers he needed. The dockyard gates would shut and the leftovers would gradually drift off with no wages to take home. And, of course, these men were older, with wives and fairly large families.

Jesus tells a similar story of day labourers hoping for work. The vineyard owner chooses the men he needs and agrees to take them on for a specific wage. Those not chosen hang around. It is usually a waste of time but they have nowhere else to go. This time they got lucky. Three hours into the working day the owner found that he needed more workers so he chose some of them and promised to pay them a fair wage.

It was clearly a very long working day. At noon and again at three in the afternoon the owner was out looking for more men. Surely there was no point hanging around after that.

But men did and 'an hour before sunset' the owner took on the last bunch. At the end of the working day the owner told his steward to pay the men, beginning with those who were employed last and ending with the first.

Every labourer received a full day's wages.

Needless to say, those who had slaved away all day long in the hot sun were not best pleased. Surely they were entitled to more than those who had worked only for a short time.

The owner said, 'My friend, I am not being unfair to you. You agreed on the usual wage for the day. . . I choose to pay the last man the same as you. . . Why be jealous because I am kind?'

As we saw with the dockers, those who only worked for an hour will have had just the same need for a decent wage as those who had been lucky enough to be employed for the whole day.

The next story I want to look at is a great favourite with anyone who ever gets to know anything about Jesus. It is the one with which I began this book – the one no one in my brother's class recognised – the story of 'the Good Samaritan'. This is to be found in Luke's Gospel (chapter ten). It begins with a famous summary of the Jewish Law which is the bedrock of decent religion.

'Love the Lord your God with all your heart, with all your soul, with all your strength and with all your mind, and your neighbour as yourself.'

Jesus is asked, 'And who is my neighbour?'

The story Jesus tells in answer to that question is significant at a number of different levels.

At its simplest it is the story of human kindness shown to a man in need – exceptional kindness. But the characters in the story make it quite clear that this is no simple story just to be taken at face value.

First of all it is significant for the people who offer help. A man has been robbed and left half dead. Two exceptionally religious men pass by and see the man lying there in need. 'They pass by on the other side.'

I remember many years ago chatting with a Hindu Brahmin. His wife was ill. Naturally you would expect him to care for her. But no, he couldn't go near her, not even into the room where she lay, because to touch her would make him ritually unclean.

So religion is no help when it comes to making people good neighbours – and it can even be a hindrance. What is needed is ordinary, common or garden decency. And where is that decency to come from?

Here is the sting in Jesus' tale. Help comes from a despised and hated foreigner – a Samaritan.

And at once our attitude to migrants, or even to the foreigner in our midst, is challenged and called into question. We are forced to face up to our own attitudes and to ask in a much more comprehensive way 'Who is my neighbour?'

There are other stories/parables in the gospels. Many of them challenge our attitudes and some of them will make us want to challenge Jesus' own attitudes, but insofar as they make us think about our own values and the way we live our lives they still have a worth in a secular age.

I want to end this chapter with three stories *about* Jesus – not stories he told but stories others told about him.

The first is in Luke chapter 7 beginning at verse 36. A Pharisee called Simon invited him to dinner. But he didn't treat Jesus as he should have treated a guest. He offered none of the usual courtesies when Jesus arrived: simply led him straight to his place at the table.

But a 'a woman who was living an immoral life' came and took her place behind him, by his feet, weeping. 'His feet were wetted with her tears and she wiped them with her hair, kissing them and anointing them with 'oil of myrrh which she had brought with her.'

Simon the Pharisee was scandalised and said to himself, 'If this fellow were a real prophet. he would know who this woman is that touches him and what sort of woman she is: a sinner.'

But of course Jesus does know. He points out to Simon the fact that he had failed in his duties as a host, showing none of the usual courtesies to his guest, but the woman had more than made up for his deficiencies. And then he says, 'her great love proves that her many sins have been forgiven.'

That really put the cat among the pigeons. 'Who does he think he is? How dare he claim to forgive sins? Only God can forgive sins' and so on. But he isn't bothered by their reactions. He is only concerned with the woman who came to him in such distress. He sends her away with the words, 'Your faith has saved you, go in peace.'

There are plenty of people living 'immoral' lives who are perfectly decent people, hardened perhaps and made somewhat cynical by the lives they lead, but perfectly decent, good, kind, generous, warm, friendly people. Demonised by society they live out of the public eye, marry, have families and have no remorse for living the way they do – sometimes the way they have been forced to take up.

Only a few end up as distressed as the woman in this story. She is not alone. There are people in all sorts of walks of life who suffer condemnation or who condemn themselves and break down, feeling that they are wicked sinners. Sometimes they need psychiatric care but sometimes all that they need is the assurance that their 'sins' are forgiven and the slate is wiped clean. Priestly absolution does not need to come from a priest. Sometimes a husband or wife will do! But forgiveness does need to come with enough authority to convince the distressed person that it is real.

Once, when I was a very young chaplain of a mental hospital, I came across a patient who was the organist at a local Baptist chapel.

He had married a girl who was brought up a Roman Catholic. When they told her priest that they wished to get married he urged the man to convert to Catholicism. The man was not interested. Ultimately the two of them married in the Baptist chapel. The priest came to see them and damned them to hell – literally.

They got on with their lives, had a very happy marriage and then the wife died. Suddenly all that the priest had said came back to haunt the widower. Could he really have caused his lovely wife to be refused entry into heaven? Had she really gone to hell? He broke down.

We chatted quietly. I didn't tell him what I *thought*. I told him with the absolute authority of a cocky young man, what a wicked sinner that priest had been and how wrong he had been. Then I took the man to the hospital chapel, bade him kneel and told him with that same authority that whatever sins he had committed were forgiven and that his wife was in heaven waiting for him.

Within a week the doctors had discharged him and he had gone home.

Often, when Jesus told people that their sins were forgiven, he went on to say 'go and sin no more.' Is it significant that on this occasion all that he says is 'Your faith has saved you. Go in peace.' Does he know that she has no alternative to the life she has been leading?

The second of these stories about Jesus that I want to mention is a story of a Samaritan woman. Samaritans feature quite often in the gospels – always to their credit. Always? Yes, even in this one.

Jesus is in Samaria, tired and thirsty, sitting by a well but with no means of drawing water from the well. A Samaritan woman comes to the well and Jesus asks her for a drink. She is surprised that a Jew would deign to speak to her on two counts: first of all, she is a mere woman (!) and secondly, she is a Samaritan.

She gives him a drink and they get into conversation. Clearly he knows more about this woman than she realised 'You have had five husbands and the man you are living with now is not your husband.'

Now the significance of this story for me is that there is no word of criticism or condemnation. Elsewhere in the gospels Jesus can be so judgemental and pretty ferocious in his damnations, but here there is just the simple statement of fact. Perhaps he has begun to learn to take his own teaching seriously: 'Judge not, that you be not judged.'

The other story is another one about not judging and it shows very clearly why we should not judge other people. It is a story that almost didn't get into the Bible at all. The translators of the New English Bible even went to the extreme of taking it out of the Gospel of John because originally it wasn't there. It was added early on in the history of the formation of the gospels – and if you know the story you will readily acknowledge that it deserves to be told as one of Jesus' finest moments. It takes place in the temple in Jerusalem.

The religious authorities brought a woman who had committed adultery to him. (Notice that it is a woman who is brought to him. The man is not.) The authorities point out something he would have known perfectly well:

'In the law Moses has laid down that such women are to be stoned' (to death). 'What do you say about it?'

Oh boy! They have got him. If he agrees with the Law, a pretty ferocious law, many people will be unhappy with him. But if he goes against it, then he is putting himself above Moses, one of the greatest men in all of their history, the man to whom God revealed his law.

But Jesus was more than a match for them. He said, 'That one of you who is faultless shall throw the first stone.' 'One by one they went away,' until Jesus was left alone, with the woman still standing there.

'Has no one condemned you?'

'No one, sir.'

'No more do I. You may go; do not sin again.'

So; he does not condone adultery. Far from it. But I find that I want to underline four of his words and print them in capitals.

'Has no one condemned you?'

'No one, sir,'

'NO MORE DO I.'

We are far too ready to condemn other people's behaviour. Perhaps if we were more aware of our own faults and weaknesses we might be a little more patient and understanding with other people.

There is a great deal in the story of Jesus which has no relevance for a secular age but in his life and in his stories he has things to say to us all.

Chapter 12

John's Gospel

If you read the gospels of Matthew and Luke you begin with stories – lovely in their way, but stories nonetheless.

And then if you continue with those two gospels, or with Mark, you read about the ministry of a wandering teacher and healer. There are healings, teachings and a miracle or two thrown in for good measure. And although at the time a good deal of his work proved to be very divisive, the casual reader can pick 'n' mix, taking whatever seems to be of value and leaving the rest.

But when you turn from these three gospels to the last of the four to be written: John's – you are in completely different territory. There is no room here for a pick 'n' mix approach. This is a gospel which tells us in no uncertain terms that we either take it or leave it, and it spells out very clearly what you are taking or leaving.

Written with great beauty and clarity, it begins with specific claims for Jesus and it continues with Jesus making the same sort of claims for himself. And always it faces us with a very clear choice, either we believe those claims and enter into the Kingdom of heaven or we do not believe and stay outside ('where there is wailing and gnashing of teeth').

It all seems very simple and straightforward. We'll look at those claims, and then ask whether the choice is really as straightforward as it seems or whether the whole thing raises questions which many of us will find insuperable.

As we have seen, the gospel begins with the claim that Jesus is 'the Word of God': 'Is', not speaks. John points out at once that 'the Word of God' is not something limited to a life of thirty odd years. It is everlasting, from everlasting to everlasting. So, if Jesus is the Word of God, he is not just a man but he is also everlasting. As the Word of God, he is divine – or as later theologians would put it, the second person of the Trinity. That claim is soon to be put into other language and enhanced: For the Jews the supreme authority was the Law of God given to Moses and interpreted by their religious leaders ever since. But John claims that Jesus goes beyond the Law.

'The Law was given through Moses, grace and truth came through Jesus Christ.' Just as the other gospels do, John begins with the ministry of John the Baptist. John's claim for Jesus is that he 'is the Lamb of God. It is he who takes away the sin of the world. This is God's Chosen One.'

But now we are shown just what these claims mean.

'He who puts his faith in the Son has hold of eternal life, but he who disobeys the Son shall not see that life. *God's wrath rests upon him.*'

This is underlined in chapter 3 when Jesus speaks with Nicodemus, and leads us to one of the favourite verses for Christians in the whole of the Bible.

Jesus says that 'unless a man has been born over again he cannot see the Kingdom of God. No one can enter the Kingdom of God without being born from water and spirit. You must be born again.'

That idea of spiritual rebirth is fundamental. We are all defined as sinners in need of salvation, a salvation which can come *only* from Jesus and which begins when we believe in him. That favourite verse of which I spoke reads:

'God loved the world so much that he gave his only Son that everyone who has faith in him may not die but have eternal life.'

But the problems begin at once. John claims 'it was not to judge the world that God sent his Son into the world but that through him the world might be saved.'

One wonders how you can possibly imagine that a message proclaimed in a tiny little bit of a small middle eastern country can be said to save 'the world' especially as 'the world' of people had been around for a long, long time already.

This question remains and will grow as we continue to look at the claims made, but we'll leave it for the time. John tells us that 'the light has come into the world. The honest man comes to the light that it may be clearly seen that God is in all he does.' However 'men preferred darkness to light.'

Up to this point, all the claims have been about Jesus, claims made by other people. From this point onwards he makes the claims for himself. And the first comes in a conversation with a woman who is twice without the pale, a story I have already mentioned: first she is a 'Samaritan woman of Sychar' – a foreigner – 'the Jews have no dealings with Samaritans', perhaps all the more so because they are racially related to one another.

Secondly, she is a woman who has had five husbands and is living with a man who is not her husband.

It is to this woman (in John's Gospel) that Jesus reveals

the 'truth' about himself before ever revealing himself to anyone else. He neither criticises her, nor judges her. We simply have his own claim that he precedes both Jewish worship (in the Temple) and Samaritan worship. She says:

'I know that Messiah is coming.'

'I am he.'

And so the claims began.

He called God his Father and claimed a special relationship with God as his Son, making it quite clear that he was the Son in a way that was different from any other human relationship with God. But he also claimed that he would make those who believed in him sons and daughters of God too.

Realising that 'by calling God his own Father he claimed equality with God' the Jews determined to kill him for blasphemy.

Jesus responded to this by raising the bar and making it quite clear that he *did* claim divine authority. This led on to the first of his famous claims: 'I am the bread of life.' Other claims were, 'I am the Light of the World'; 'I am the Good Shepherd'; 'I am the door of the sheepfold', and the last was, 'I am the Resurrection and the Life.'

These claims shocked many people. His own brothers did not believe in him. But the same claims have given many Christians huge inspiration and comfort over the centuries.

Whilst I do not believe those claims it would be quite wrong to undervalue what belief in Jesus has meant for many, many people. He had, and for some he still has, the power to enrich and inspire their lives. They are not interested in nit-picking questions of theology or in credal correctness. They only know that through his life and teachings Jesus has enriched and inspired them.

Those of us who do not believe in him should recognise all this and respect him for the good his inspiration still achieves.

We should perhaps notice that according to this gospel Jesus spent a great deal more time in Jerusalem than the other gospels suggest. How true this is we cannot know but John says that it was his brothers who pointed out to Jesus that if he wanted to make a real impression it was not enough just to travel around Galilee. He had to make his mark in Jerusalem.

According to John it was these visits to Jerusalem that built hostility between Jesus and the authorities. One example of that hostility is to be found in the wonderful story in chapter nine. The story is about a man who had been blind and was healed by Jesus but that is not why I called it a wonderful story. The Pharisees tried to undermine people's reactions to Jesus saying, 'We know that this man is a sinner.' They questioned both the blind man and his parents. But it is the healed man whose response to the Pharisees catches our attention ending his response to them with:

'What an extraordinary thing! He is a man who has opened my eyes, yet you do not know where he comes from! . . . If that man had not come from God he could have done nothing.'

Whatever we think of Jesus this story of the confrontation of the healed man and the Pharisees is a joy to read.

Chapter 13

Resurrection

John chapter eleven has the story of the raising of Lazarus from the dead. It goes into great detail. And there is the suggestion that Jesus delayed responding to appeals from his friends Martha and Mary for help deliberately so that he could be seen to have power over death.

Belief in resurrection was common, often with people being thought of as a kind of reincarnation. People thought of John the Baptist as Elijah come back from the dead. And it was not only Herod who thought that Jesus was John the Baptist come back from the dead.

Throughout the ministry of Jesus his followers kept on claiming that he had raised people from death and it was usually Jesus himself who stressed that the claims were not true. Jairus' daughter is a case in point. People said that she was dead. Jesus said, 'She is not dead. She is asleep.'

So what are we to make of the story of Lazarus? According to the story he had been in the tomb for four days before Jesus raised him. The whole story was told to enshrine his claim: 'I am the resurrection and I am life.' He went on to say that those who had faith in him would never die.

Clearly his claim was not that those who believe in him would live for ever on earth. It was a promise that they would live for ever in paradise.

But what are we to make of the story itself? It raises a host of questions beginning with the question of how gullible the author was? If he could believe this story, it is no wonder that he could believe all the other supernatural claims he makes for Jesus. And if Jesus really made these claims, how can we give much credence to him either?

Humans are animals – rather unusual animals in some respects, and very distinctive animals – very destructive animals, too – but animals, nonetheless. Like all other animals, they are born, they live and they die. That is the end of the story.

So what are we to make of poor old Lazarus – a man of whom we know next to nothing. If the story was true he was raised from death to live out his anonymous life and then to die again. Lucky man.

If there is any truth in the story, then Lazarus was one of those poor unfortunates who was buried alive. I'm not sure of my facts but I remember reading once that (was it) about one in one hundred and twenty of those who were buried in the time of Jesus had been mis-diagnosed as dead. They were buried alive!

We shall, of course, come to this question of resurrection again when we reach the death of Jesus himself. There are those who have suggested that he did not really die on the cross but I am not one of them. What followed the crucifixion was incredibly simple and it is all there in the Gospel of Matthew. Yet oddly, I have never known of anybody else who has noticed the truth expressed there.

The simple truth is that Jesus did not rise from death and it is my own belief that he did not raise Lazarus from death either.

Chapter 14

The Path to Crucifixion

We are drawing close to the end of the story. It poses a host of questions and contains some of the most sublime teaching of all and moments of sheer bathos such as Peter swinging his sword and cutting off the ear of the high priest's servant.

Let us begin with the teaching. It is to be found in John's Gospel from late on in chapter twelve to the end of chapter seventeen. Early in it all comes the famous incident where he washes the feet of his followers. He told them to wash one another's feet and sometimes Christian leaders take it into their heads to re-enact this scene.

In the fourteenth chapter there are some of the most beautiful and comforting words you will find anywhere – comforting to those who believe them. Read the whole chapter but especially verses one to six and 27. What could be lovelier than verse 27.

'Peace is my parting gift to you, my own peace such as the world cannot give. Set your troubled hearts at rest, and banish your fears.'

It is also in these chapters that you will find a great deal of his teaching about love and in his final prayer for his followers he prays again and again that they will love one another, because it is through their love that they will demonstrate to the rest of us that his teaching is true.

Sadly, the story of his followers never has been one of 'love'. Instead it has been all too human. There was bickering from the start and the whole story right through Christian history has been one of splintering and division. Jesus said (according to John) 'the time is coming when anyone who kills you will suppose that he is fulfilling a religious duty.' Frankly, there is no institution that has done more killing, regarding it as a religious duty, than the churches. If I had lived four hundred years ago and written the things I have been writing in this book, I would have been burned at the stake. (It wouldn't have happened because I'm much too cowardly or sensible to have put my life on the line in such a way!)

It is also in chapter seventeen, in the first few verses, that we find the central claim upon which all of Jesus' authority lies, but it only has meaning for those who believe it. There is also a good deal of teaching in these chapters about the third person of the Christian divine trinity: the Holy Spirit. The Spirit was supposed to be going to enter into the hearts and lives of the followers of Jesus to enable them to continue his ministry.

Very occasionally you will find people, not just within Christianity but in all faiths and none, who seem to have a quality which sets them aside from the rest of us. It is rare. But very occasionally we find people who seem to have a depth of understanding and a quality that most of us can only dream of. Religious people may feel that such people are filled with the Spirit of God. I prefer to think that they are filled with the spirit of humanity at its best.

Sadly, that kind of quality only marks the followers of Jesus very rarely. For the rest – they are no different from any of the rest of us.

From these chapters in John's Gospel we turn to the story of the activities of the last week of Jesus' life, and again and again I find myself asking the question 'why?'. Why did Jesus behave as he did? What was he trying to achieve? If he had been so minded, he could have gone on with his life as a wandering teacher indefinitely. But he wasn't so minded. According to the gospels he said that he must be arrested and killed and (again according to the gospels) he said that he would rise again on the third day from his death. And the point of it all? He was giving his life 'as a ransom for many.'

I want to look at that idea separately in a chapter about the Christian ideas concerning salvation.

Here let us simply look at the story and the way in which Jesus seems to have sought confrontation and almost forced the authorities into arresting him.

The story begins triumphantly with him riding into Jerusalem on a donkey (a sign that he came in peace. Warriors rode horses). Surrounded by those who knew him from Galilee, it was like a celebration – a sort of May Day bank holiday or a Notting Hill festival – all very good humoured and delightful.

But the following day it all turned sour. Jesus led a demonstration. In the temple precincts there were traders selling birds and animals for sacrifice in the temple. If you brought your own sacrifice it was often turned down as imperfect so that you were forced to buy from the market traders at vastly inflated prices. Jesus led a demonstration against them, driving them all out – no doubt plenty of his

d

followers joined in when he began. It had all the excitement, righteous anger and emotion of any demo – and it was just as pointless. The market traders would have been back the following day. Whereas our police would have made a few arrests on the day, his behaviour only led the authorities to begin thinking along those lines.

There were more parables – not particularly pleasant or enlightening ones, such as the story of the 'foolish' virgins who were shut out of a wedding, or the story of the talents.

But perhaps the most significant teaching, which fills a chapter in the first three gospels, was the prophecy of the destruction of Jerusalem and its temple. But I suspect that this was not the teaching of Jesus at all. It was probably prophecy after the event, like most prophecy in the Bible, it is a pretty devastating chapter. It has been used by fringe groups on the edges of Christianity, such as the Jehovah's Witnesses, to warn us of the end of time and the final judgement of God when those accepted by God will find their ultimate joy and the rest of us will be doomed.

'Nation will make war upon nation, kingdom upon kingdom, there will be great earthquakes and famines and plagues in many places; in the sky terrors and great portents.' (Luke 21-10 and 11).

Those are fairly obvious prophecies that anyone can make. But in fact Jerusalem *was* destroyed, including its temple, first by Titus in (I think) 70 CE and then in the 140s by the Romans more comprehensively.

For the next couple of days the authorities were content to debate with Jesus and to try to trap him into saying things which would have been grounds for his arrest and execution. But he was a match for them and eventually, at night, after the last supper, under cover of darkness, assisted by his follower Judas Iscariot, they did arrest him.

The gospels have the story of his trial before the priests and before Pilate and Herod. The words of Caiaphas are the most significant of all:

'It is more to your interest that one man should die for the people than that the whole nation should be destroyed.'

He obviously felt that Jesus posed some sort of revolutionary threat which would bring down the wrath of Rome on them.

Eventually and apparently unwillingly, Pilate condemned him to death and he was crucified.

The story of the crucifixion deserves to be treated with sensitivity. However misguided Jesus may have been in these last days, crucifixion was a cruel kind of execution. The soldiers around him show a good deal of the nastiness of which we are capable. Jesus himself is both courageous and dignified. There is a moment when he seems at first sight to have descended into complete despair:

'My God, my God, why hast thou forsaken me?'

But those words are a quotation from a psalm which ends in triumph, so they may not be as despairing as they sound. Certainly, he sounded much more at peace with his situation when he told one of those crucified with him, 'today you shall be with me in Paradise.'

His mother was the only member of his family to be present at the crucifixion and there is a tender moment when Jesus committed her into the care of his disciple John.

After his death two significant Jews, Joseph of Arimathea and Nicodemus obtained permission to take him and bury him in a rock tomb with a great stone rolled against its entrance.

And then what happened?

'There was an earthquake, the rocks split, and the graves opened. . . And when the centurion and his men. . . saw the earthquake. . . they were filled with awe.'

The Revd. Frank Pagden has pointed out that the area is prone to earthquakes. And all of us who saw on TV the earthquakes which devastated both Turkey and Syria in 2022 will recognise what they can do.

The first women to visit the tomb of Jesus 'finding that the stone had been rolled away from the tomb, they went inside, but the body was not to be found. . .' It was lost to the earthquake. The story (of the resurrection) 'appeared to them to be nonsense and they would not believe' those who told it.

But others were more gullible. They were not alone. After the death of John the Baptist, Herod and others thought that Jesus was John the Baptist risen from the dead. Some people will believe anything, as modern stories of weeping statues or coronation 'holy oil' make very clear. And so stories began to be told just as stories began to be told of the birth of Jesus – sometimes quite lovely stories, but stories nonetheless.

And there are plenty of modern Christians who have a problem with those stories of a physical resurrection of Jesus and who explain them away. The real resurrection was not the physical resurrection of Jesus but the rise of the Christian churches – just as incredible in its way.

Chapter 15

Not the Virtuous but Sinners

I was brought up to believe that we all need Jesus. We are *all* sinners in need of salvation and without Jesus salvation is impossible.

Salvation brings us into the family of God as the children of God. Without salvation we are doomed.

But Jesus himself doesn't seem to have believed that we all need him.

Jesus said that he didn't come to call the virtuous to follow him. Does this mean that he recognised that there are people who are virtuous? Evangelical preachers seem to think not. We are all sinners in need of salvation.

And salvation involves the perfect sacrifice of Jesus the Lamb of God. First we have to repent of our sins and then we have to put our faith in the sacrifice of Jesus so that he can ransom us from the slavery of sin and bring us into the family of God.

But that on its own is not enough. It leads to the reward of life after death in heaven – perpetual bliss. Whereas those who are not saved go to hell and eternal damnation.

I have put this as starkly as I can. It is pretty much the

message preached again and again when I was young. It poses a multitude of questions and problems.

Jesus painted a picture of human beings as sheep and goats. The sheep went to heaven. The goats went to hell. This poses the question, are we sheep (tails down) or goats (tails up). Can people really be divided so clearly into two camps?

We are none of us perfect. Some of us are pretty wonderful and some of us can be horrible, but where do you draw the line?

And what of all those people who have never heard of Jesus? Just think about it. Jesus spent two or three of his thirty odd years leaving the virtuous alone and calling sinners. He called a few thousand sinners in a little country in the Middle East. He was unknown to millions of people who had lived for how many thousands of years before he was born. He was unknown to many more millions of people who have lived since he was born. He is unknown or virtually unknown to many millions of people who are alive today. And most of those who do know anything about him, know comparatively little about him.

Are all of those people doomed just because they have never heard of him? The very idea is crazy.

And what of that 'doom'? Evangelical preachers loved going on about it. But it was Jesus himself who began it. Some of his most horrible teaching involved pronouncing woes on whole towns such as Bethsaida and Chorazin. He was the one who produced the ideas of the judgement of God separating people into sheep and goats. (Why did he have it in for goats I wonder?)

I don't think many people in this country believe in either heaven or hell any more. We make our own heavens and our own hells in this life without any need for another. Perhaps a few cling on to some sort of vague hope of heaven or of reunion with loved ones. My father had ideas of going back to school to prepare for heaven and then of meeting wonderful people like Shakespeare – without ever asking himself whether Shakespeare would be interested in meeting him.

As for hell, I don't think that holds any terrors any more. Most people just don't believe in it.

I'm now in my nineties. I've met an awful lot of people in my lifetime – a few of them in prison for various offences. I have never yet met anybody I would consign to hell. And if I wouldn't, how could a loving God? The very idea is preposterous rubbish.

But then, the whole idea of rewards in heaven and hell is rubbish too. If salvation into the family of God in this life is not enough, it is pretty pathetic. Salvation from a life of sin into a life of virtue within the family of God should be sufficient in itself. If it is not, it has little value.

But the very idea of salvation through a perfect sacrifice poses a host of questions and problems. The first of them again is that question, how many of us are really bad enough to need saving? When Jesus said that he didn't come to call the virtuous but sinners, where did he draw the line? Who is a sheep and who is a goat?

To believe in the Christian teaching about salvation you have to believe that you are a wicked sinner. You have to believe that there is a God and that this incredible being is interested in a tiny, insignificant individual like any one of us. You have to believe that Jesus was perfect, where the gospel evidence shows clearly that he was not – that he both was a perfect sacrifice and is the second person of the godhead. You have to believe that this God-man sacrificed himself to himself for little me.

You have to believe that you are so very significant that you are worth such a sacrifice – and is that kind of belief in our own significance not evidence in itself of overweening pride?

It is no wonder that theologians have spent so much time trying to provide a satisfactory theology of salvation and have never really managed to satisfy either themselves or anybody else.

But if we set this idea of salvation on one side is there no value in becoming a follower of Jesus the teacher? When I was a boy an evangelist taught us that the secret of joy is to put:

J esus first

O thers second and

Y ourself last.

It was a very simple and attractive idea. I'm quite sure that for many people it is true that if they become Christians they will become better people. But it is probably equally true that if people become Jewish by faith, or Hindus, Buddhists, Confucians, Epicureans, Stoics or Moslems or any of a dozen or more faiths or philosophies, it is possible that they will become better people.

Let us go back to the very beginning. Jesus said that he came not to call the virtuous but sinners. Although none of us is perfect, very few of us are really bad. Most of us are not sinful enough for anybody to make a fuss about it. Most of us are pretty decent people on the whole, warm, friendly, helpful and kind. We do our best for our families and for one another, and even reach out beyond our close acquaintances towards others in need.

And even those of us who are seriously bad cannot be made good by anybody else. They can be inspired to change – yes by a Jesus, but more likely by the love and quality of someone near to them. But in the end they themselves are the ones who must achieve radical change in themselves. Each individual is responsible for his or her own life. No one can stand in as a substitute.

If we are seriously bad, then yes, we need to repent (which is to turn away from our badness) and we have to set about changing ourselves in radical ways. Others can help. The Christian gospel can help some. But in the end, change is down to ourselves. That is the supreme truth. If we will, either on our own or with help from others, if we are significantly bad, we can change. Although I don't like that picture of sheep and goats. If I'm a goat (tail up) I think I want to stay that way!

Conclusion

Unless you believe in God and his Kingdom, life after death, God's judgement, and his salvation, his separation of people into those fit for heaven and those doomed to go to hell – all those things I was brought up to believe – there is remarkably little in the gospels – in the life and teaching of Jesus – which has any relevance for life in a secular world.

The churches spawned by the Christian religion can be home to some wonderful music and beautiful works of art (as well as the opposite) but they are simply human institutions with all of our human qualities and with all of our human failings. They exist for those who like them but have no value or relevance for any of the rest of us.

As for Jesus himself: apart from his quality as a man, some of his stories and a few pithy statements, there is very little left.

The supernatural elements of the gospels and the theological wranglings ever since, they are all meaningless and worthless.

Insofar as the teaching of Jesus helps us to live better lives it has a value, but there are plenty of other teachers who are just as helpful.

'Consider the birds of the air. . . Consider the lilies of the valley. . .' they do not seem to be aware of gods or goddesses; they do not need religions, philosophies, systems of ethics, or even teachers, ancient or modem; and neither do we. Whatever value any of these may have for those who are devoted to them, they are all optional extras. Masses of people get along perfectly well without them and most of these people live lives that are virtuous on the whole, valuable and valued. And when their lives are over, people like me conduct their funerals.

The Legacy

There was a carpenter of Nazareth
who died an awful death
but left a legacy of love
which warmed the hearts of those he left.

No matter what the life we live,
no matter what the death we die,
no matter whether rich or poor,
if we can leave a legacy of love
which warms the hearts of those we love
our lives have been worthwhile.